Arise and Abide Volume 1

Copyright 2020 LaToya Moulton
All rights reserved. No part of this book may be used or reproduced by any means, graphic, electronic, or mechanical, including photocopying, recording, taping or by any information storage retrieval system without the written permission of the publisher. Copying this book is both illegal and unethical.

ISBN print: 978-0-578-69971-4

Library of Congress Control Number
Categories: Fiction/Christian Living
Printed in the United States of America

Unless otherwise indicated, Scripture quotations are taken from the King James Version (KJV), New King James Version (NKJV), New Living Translation (NLT), New International Version (NIV), and Amplified Version (AMP). All rights reserved.

Contents

Introduction 1

With This Journal You Will Find 7

Self Examination 11

Life Application & L.E.A.N In Process 15

Invitation To Journal 32

To you reader,

May your roots run deep.

May your life forever thrive.

Introduction

Over the years I've learned—and yet still continuing to learn how to embrace and accept the following words as a part of my identity: redeemed, forgiven, beautiful, whole, worthy, capable, called, chosen and most importantly, His. That I belong to God. I am loved by God. And that I am seen by God. I cling and choose to stand on these words daily as a part of my restored identity. However, I didn't always make these declarations of truth my own. For many years, I carried the shame of my past like a heavy weight of baggage on my back. It completely hindered me from showing up as the highest version of myself, which my Creator had predestined me to be.

If I could be honest, I just lacked the understanding, I did not know how deeply loved I was. Actually, I felt deeply hurt and scattered to the side like damaged goods, unnoticed, and labeled as a lost cause. This was the story I constantly rehearsed to myself. Unfortunately, I didn't understand then as I do now that this persuasive narrative was a concoction of lies designed by the enemy of my soul to destroy me. He didn't want me to know how loved, favored, and powerful I really was.

Precious reader maybe you can relate, is there some form of baggage holding you down? Or is there a nagging negative narrative on replay in the back of your mind? And this negative narrative has your ankles ensnared which is hindering you from fully running your race and showing up big for your life. What lies has the enemy been whispering to you? You're not good enough? You're not worthy? It's too late for you? Things will never change or get better for you? Oh! How these lies have a way of distorting our God-vision and eating away at the foundation of our identity. The enemy of our souls is crafty and deceives many of us by whispering lies that almost sound like truth if we lack the understanding of who we really are. His ammunition of choice is the trauma and pain we experience. He tries to ensnare us with the pain of our past, the smoke screens of doubt concerning our present, and the intimidating filters of bleakness related to our future. He lies to us with hopes that we would abandon the path God has us on, disregard and bury our talents, disown our dreams, lose sight of our vision, and discourage us so much until we lose hope. He cons us into being so busy we disregard what really matters. We become so self-sufficient we feel no need to cast our cares on God even though He asks us to do so daily. The enemy whispers so loudly we tend to forget what Jesus said, "Are you tired and heavy laden? Come learn of me. My yoke is easy and my burden is light." God never intended for us to carry life's burdens alone—better yet—to carry them at all.

I was in need of resuscitation. My dreams, talents, potential—all that God had purposed for me laid lifeless within. Then one day, in the midst of my broken, scattered pieces, redemption and restoration came knocking at my door. The One who calls Himself the Resurrection and the Life spoke to me with such great compassion and tender care. He said, *"Talitha Cumi,* damsel arise for nothing will be wasted." I had no idea

God was inviting me to a vast table of abundance. It was a warm and gracious invitation to sit and feast with Him daily. In His presence, I learned to draw from the well that never runs dry, how to lean in, and hear the songs of deliverance being sung over me. The holiness of God would surround me and the water of His Holy Word washing over me. And today reader as your reading these words I sense a *Talitha Cumi* for you as well. This is your invitation!

Only in His presence feasting on His Word did transformation begin to take place. Mine was the type of transformation that calls you forth from the place of worry to a position of worship. It rightfully restores the broken pieces of your shattered identity, takes you from the pit of despair and puts you in an established place of confidence and praise. It was the type of transformation that shifts you from a position of fear to a place of faith, that revives purpose and brings forth clarity of vision.

Sprouts of truth sprung up in my soul declaring: "I am not damaged goods. I am no victim. I am no beggar sitting on the floor pleading for crumbs. I am His! Forgiven. Deeply loved. Crowned with favor. God is my Father; therefore, I carry a part of Him within me. It is eternal. It is holy."

As I have sojourned walking through these different seasons of growth – and there were many times when He carried me as well. I've discovered that our Heavenly Father longs to refresh our souls daily. He is deeply concerned about everything that concerns you. In the busyness of life when you find yourself striving, comparing, reaching, longing, and accomplishing, He wants to renew, refresh, and revive you.

When you arise from momentary satisfaction to only find yourself thirsty again, He is there to restore.

Do you want to fill the void in your life and discover your identity? Are you desperate to quench the thirst in your soul? Would you like to experience a life-changing awakening?

Over the years, I allowed my roots to run deeper feasting on the Word of God. Gradually, with much grace and the tender process of growth and time, I witnessed new life springing up, not only within but around me. And here is your invite – you can too! An inner transformation was taking place within my soul. My mind was being renewed and my dormant dreams revved up. Fresh brooks of revival were bubbling up and flowing in, out of, and around me causing a ripple effect of change, encouragement, and empowerment to others. A new sense of self-love, identity, self-worth, and clarity of vision was springing up. Here in this place I had an epiphany that "there is no pit too deep beyond God's reach, there is no mess that He cannot birth forth a message from, and there is no wondering soul too far gone He cannot rescue". He Redeems. He Restores. And I am declaring this unto you today!

One of the key transformational components of sitting at the table of vast abundance is the willingness to bring all of who you are. Yes, you heard me correctly bring ALL of you to the table. And that during this time of feasting be willing to surrender your dreams, ideas, passions ambitions, concerns, fears, doubts, requests, longings, uncertainties into the hands of a Trustworthy God who cares for you completely. Lay it on the table. And as doing so when you surrender, you must open your heart and hands to receive. Receive the bountifulness of His goodness, mercy, forgiveness, favor, truth filled life speaking promises that are only YES and AMEN that we can confidently stand upon victoriously no matter what storm we may encounter in this life. He is the anchor that will cause us to weather it all. As I walk you through this prayer journal approach this sacred time alone with God not as an obligation but look at it more as a personal invitation from our Heavenly Father who longs to spend time with you. It is not to be checked off our religious famous to-do list but welcomed as an intimate beckoning to sit and allow the Holy Spirit to refill and refresh you. As women, wives, singles, mothers, daughters, sisters, friends, career women, business owners, leaders whatever your sphere of influence may be that the Lord has strategically positioned you - My prayer is you will allow the Lover of your soul to fill your cup and let it overflow! Arise and meet each day! Abide and feast at the table of God's abundance. He has so much more in store for you—so lean in.

With This Journal You Will Find

Four Sections Included:

1. **Self Examination:** you'll take an inside look at how you view your relationship with God and His Word.
2. **Journal:** 80+ pages for you to journal your thoughts, prayers and what God is saying to you. For each day there will be a different meditational scripture at the end of each page to give you something to ponder and meditate upon.
3. **Prayer Prompt Questions:** a guided prayer prompt question that will help you dive a little deeper during your time of response and receiving.
4. **Life Application:** learn the process I created called L.E.A.N in. An application skill created to show you how to apply the scripture to your life for optimal transformation.

I hope this journal becomes a tool which will help you Grow in God and Thrive in Life.

Spiritual growth is like learning to walk. We stand up, fall, stand up, fall, take a step, fall, take a couple of steps, fall, walk a little better, wobble a bit, fall, run, and finally, we eventually fly then we learn how to soar.

Self Examination

HOW DO YOU DEFINE YOUR RELATIONSHIP WITH GOD AND HIS WORD?

_____
_____
_____
_____
_____

ON A SCALE FROM 1 TO 10 WITH 10 BEING THE HIGHEST. RATE YOUR LEVEL OF RELATIONSHIP.

1 2 3 4 5 6 7 8 9 10

WHY DID YOU GIVE YOUR RELATIONSHIP THIS RATING?

_____
_____
_____
_____

ARE YOU SATISFIED WITH WHERE YOUR RELATIONSHIP IS RIGHT NOW?

_____

WHAT IS GOD SAYING TO ME ABOUT MY RELATIONSHIP WITH HIM AND HIS WORD?

Scripture References & Life Application

L.E.A.N

In the busyness of life from the many different roles we fill as women carving out the time to slow down and intentionally create that space to make sure we fill our cups are vital. There are many times when we read the scripture it's so easy to get caught up with the mindset of checking it off of our "to do list". That we miss the divine invitation to sit and feast off the delicacy of God's Promises given to us. Not slowing down long enough to really see how it should be applied to our lives – reading His Word alone simply for head knowledge does not produce true growth and transformation. But it is the sitting, pressing, meditating upon, praying it through, asking the Holy Spirit to speak and reveal and being willing with a receptive heart to receive what the Father desires to bestow upon us.

This is where transformation, healing, restoration, and renewal for the soul takes place! In this section, I will teach you the simply process I created called L.E.A.N IN. Below is the explanation for the acronym. We have provided you the opportunity to the read the bible verses and see how simple and easy the process called L.E.A.N IN can be applied to scripture and to your life!

L: look up; any words that jump out to you. Circle them, place a square around it, underline it, highlight

E: examin; look over the scripture once, twice. Look up definitions of certain words that resonate with you. Park your pace, slow down and sit with the word

A: accept; take in the Truth of Gods Word as your own. Make it personal. Receive what the Father has for you. Journal out your prayers, confessions, pour out your heart to Him. Write out a declaration of acceptance and openly declare it over your life!

N: nourish; in what ways could you tend to the soil of your heart as the seed of truth takes root? One key is to receive truth with faith and trust that what His Word declares is your portion. Remember we have an enemy who is a thief (John 10:10) and one of his main objectives is to immediately steal the truth seed once we plant it into the soil of our hearts. Examples that could help you nourish the seed of truth: Take some index cards and write out the scripture practice memorizing it place it somewhere you can see. Prayer. Praise, worship and gratitude is an excellent way to continue cultivating the soil of our hearts as we nurture the seed of truth. Daily confessions of speaking and declaring God's word over our lives. Sharing truth with others. Building relationships in a thriving healthy community just to name a few.

I have provided an example on the following page to give you an idea of how to get the most out of this section. And if you honestly take your time and do the work, it will pay off in the end. This is truly how your roots run deep and transformation takes place.

Let's get started!

PSALM 121:2

God is my Help, the Lord is the One <u>who sustains me</u>

WHAT IS THIS SCRIPTURE SAYING TO ME?

Who is my help? My help does not come from men. Or external factors even though God can use them all as instruments in aiding me. However it is the LORD ONLY who is My HELP. He is my rescue. He is my shelter. He is my ultimate source and strength. It is the LORD ONLY that preserves me; sustains me; keeps me sustain: strength or support physically or mentally; comfort, help, assistw

HOW DO I APPLY THE SCRIPTURE TO MY LIFE?

When I find myself standing against opposition, or facing any kind of challenge I do not have to fear or feel alone. The God of the universe has been and will always be my present help. Because of this truth I can run to Him for aid and He will assist me. He will sustain and support me.

ISAIAH 41:10

Don't be afraid, for I am with you. Don't' be discouraged. For I am your God. I will strengthen you and help you. I will hold you up with my victorious right hand.

WHAT IS THIS SCRIPTURE SPREAKING TO ME?

_____
_____
_____
_____
_____

HOW DO I APPLY THE SCRIPTURE TO MY LIFE?

_____
_____
_____
_____
_____

Arise: to get up from sitting down, spring forth, stand up

HOW IS GOD CALLING ME TO ARISE?

WHAT DOSE IT MEAN TO ME TO CULTIVATE HIS WORD IN MY LIFE?
(Look up the definition for the word cultivate.)

Cultivate:

Cultivate your life. Water it daily, pour some tender loving care into it, and watch it grow. Remember that a plant doesn't sprout immediately. Be patient and know that in life you will reap what you sow.

Abide: to remain stable or fixed in a state of love; to continue in a place; sojourn

HOW IS GOD CALLING ME TO ABIDE?

WHAT DOES TRANSFORMATION THROUGH THE WORD OF GOD LOOKS LIKE TO ME?
(Define the word transformation)

Transformation:

_____

_____

_____

_____

_____

_____

_____

_____

_____

_____

_____

_____

_____

_____

_____

_____

_____

_____

Transformation is a journey, not a destination.

For I, the LORD your God, hold your right hand; it is I who say to you, "Fear not, I am the One who helps you."

ISAIAH 41:13

Date: _____

Prayer and Response

Heavenly Father, today I will abide with...

But those who hope in the LORD will renew their strength. They will soar on wings like eagles; they will run and not grow weary; they will walk and not be faint.

ISAIAH 40:31

Date: _____

_____
_____
_____
_____
_____
_____
_____
_____
_____
_____
_____
_____
_____
_____
_____
_____

Prayer and Response

Heavenly Father, today I will dwell on...

_____

_____

_____

_____

_____

_____

_____

_____

_____

_____

_____

_____

_____

_____

_____

Because of the LORD's great love we are not consumed, for his compassions never fail. They are new every morning; great is your faithfulness.

LAMENTATIONS 3:22-23

Date: _____

_____
_____
_____
_____
_____
_____
_____
_____
_____
_____
_____
_____
_____
_____
_____
_____

Prayer and Response

Heavenly Father, today I will pause with...

_____
_____
_____
_____
_____
_____
_____
_____
_____
_____
_____
_____
_____
_____
_____
_____
_____

> For we are God's masterpiece, created in Christ Jesus to do good works, which God prepared in advanced for us to walk in it.
>
> EPHESIANS 2:10

Date: _____

_____
_____
_____
_____
_____
_____
_____
_____
_____
_____
_____
_____
_____
_____
_____
_____
_____

Prayer and Response

Heavenly Father, today I will linger with...

_____
_____
_____
_____
_____
_____
_____
_____
_____
_____
_____
_____
_____
_____
_____
_____
_____
_____

The LORD is my strength and my shield; my heart trusted in Him, and I was helped; therefore my heart rejoices and with my song I will thank Him.

PSALM 28:7

Date: _____

Prayer and Response

Heavenly Father, today I will rest with...

_____
_____
_____
_____
_____
_____
_____
_____
_____
_____
_____
_____
_____
_____
_____
_____
_____
_____
_____

You do not discover who you are in the presence of people. You discover who you are in the presence of God

— LISA BEVERE —

Define yourself radically as one beloved by God. This is the true self. Every other identity is an Illusion.

– BRENNAN MANNING –

Date: _____

Prayer and Response

Heavenly Father, today I will abide with...

But now, this is what the LORD says, He who created you, O Jacob, and He who formed you, O Israel: Do not fear, for I have redeemed you; I have called you by name; you are Mine.

ISAIAH 43:1

Date: _____

Prayer and Response

Heavenly Father, today I will dwell on…

_____

_____

_____

_____

_____

_____

_____

_____

_____

_____

_____

_____

_____

_____

_____

_____

> I wait for you LORD, You are my Divine Help and Impenetrable Shield.
>
> PSALM 33:20

Date: _____

_____
_____
_____
_____
_____
_____
_____
_____
_____
_____
_____
_____
_____
_____
_____
_____

Prayer and Response

Heavenly Father, today I will pause with...

_____
_____
_____
_____
_____
_____
_____
_____
_____
_____
_____
_____
_____
_____
_____
_____
_____
_____
_____

> I sought the LORD and He answered me
> and delivered me from all my fears.
>
> PSALM 34:4

Date: _____

Prayer and Response

Heavenly Father, today I will linger with...

_____
_____
_____
_____
_____
_____
_____
_____
_____
_____
_____
_____
_____
_____
_____
_____
_____

> I constantly trust in the LORD; because He is my right hand, I will not be upended.
>
> PSALM 16:8

Date: _____

Prayer and Response

Heavenly Father, today I will rest with...

_____

_____

_____

_____

_____

_____

_____

_____

_____

_____

_____

_____

_____

_____

_____

_____

> Ah Lord God! It is you who made the heavens and the earth by your great power and outstretched arm! Nothing is too hard for you
>
> JEREMIAH 32:17

Date: _____

A woman who walks with God will always reach her destination.

I AM the daughter of a King who is not moved by the world. For my God is with me and goes before me. I do not fear because I Am His.

The boundary lines have fallen for me in pleasant places. Indeed my inheritance is beautiful to me.

PSALM 16:6

Date: _____

Prayer and Response

Heavenly Father, today I will abide with...

_____

_____

_____

_____

_____

_____

_____

_____

_____

_____

_____

_____

_____

_____

_____

_____

_____

He who calls me is faithful;
He will surely do it.

1ST THESSALONIANS 5:24

Date: _____

_____
_____
_____
_____
_____
_____
_____
_____
_____
_____
_____
_____
_____
_____

Prayer and Response

Heavenly Father, today I will dwell on...

My God shall supply fill unto full my every need according to His riches in glory in Christ Jesus.

PHILIPPIANS 4:19

Date: _____

_____
_____
_____
_____
_____
_____
_____
_____
_____
_____
_____
_____
_____
_____
_____
_____
_____
_____

Prayer and Response

Heavenly Father, today I will pause with...

_____

_____

_____

_____

_____

_____

_____

_____

_____

_____

_____

_____

_____

_____

_____

_____

_____

_____

Whether you turn to the right or to the left, your will hear a voice behind you, saying, "This is the way; walk in it."

ISAIAH 30:21

Date: _____

Prayer and Response

Heavenly Father, today I will linger with…

For I know the plans I have for you, declares the LORD, plans to prosper you and not to harm you, plans to give you hope and a future. Then you will call on me and come and pray to me, and I will listen to you.

JEREMIAH 29:11-12

Date: _____

_____
_____
_____
_____
_____
_____
_____
_____
_____
_____
_____
_____
_____
_____
_____

Prayer and Response

Heavenly Father, today I will rest with...

___

I was created for a purpose with a purpose on purpose

God has placed you here for a purpose, whatever it might be. Hold to this truth He has you in the palm of hands therefore labor faithfully in this season. Bloom where you are planted.

> I know that You can do all things, no purpose of Yours can be prevented.
>
> JOB 42:2

Date: _____

_____
_____
_____
_____
_____
_____
_____
_____
_____
_____
_____
_____
_____
_____
_____
_____
_____

Prayer and Response

Heavenly Father, today I will abide with...

_____
_____
_____
_____
_____
_____
_____
_____
_____
_____
_____
_____
_____
_____
_____
_____
_____
_____

When you pass through the waters, I will be with you; and when you pass through the rivers, they will not sweep over you. When you walk through the fire, you will not be burned; the flames will not set you ablaze.

ISAIAH 43:2

Date: _____

Prayer and Response

Heavenly Father, today I will dwell on...

_____

_____

_____

_____

_____

_____

_____

_____

_____

_____

_____

_____

_____

_____

_____

_____

_____

_____

> For we live by faith,
> not by sight.
>
> 2ND CORINTHIANS 5:7

Date: _____

_____
_____
_____
_____
_____
_____
_____
_____
_____
_____
_____
_____
_____
_____
_____
_____
_____
_____
_____
_____

Prayer and Response

Heavenly Father, today I will pause with...

_____

_____

_____

_____

_____

_____

_____

_____

_____

_____

_____

_____

_____

_____

_____

_____

> My salvation and my honor depend on God;
> he is my mighty rock, my refuge.
>
> PSALM 62:7

Date: _____

Prayer and Response

Heavenly Father, today I will linger with…

_____

_____

_____

_____

_____

_____

_____

_____

_____

_____

_____

_____

_____

_____

_____

_____

_____

> Ask, and it shall be given you: seek, and you shall find; knock and the door shall be opened to you.
>
> MATTHEW 7:7

Date: _____

_____
_____
_____
_____
_____
_____
_____
_____
_____
_____
_____
_____
_____
_____
_____
_____

Prayer and Response

Heavenly Father, today I will rest with...

The Timeless Promises of God Are Our Confident Hope

I believe when we linger and sit with the Word of God this creates space for revelation and impartation. We give time to grace and truth to saturate the soil of our hearts.

— LATOYA MOULTON —

> But when you ask, you must believe and not doubt, because the one who doubts is like a wave of the sea, blown and tossed by the wind.
>
> JAMES 1:6

Date: _____

_____
_____
_____
_____
_____
_____
_____
_____
_____
_____
_____
_____
_____
_____
_____
_____
_____

Prayer and Response

Heavenly Father, today I will abide with...

_____

_____

_____

_____

_____

_____

_____

_____

_____

_____

_____

_____

_____

_____

_____

> He will not let your foot slip—he who watches over you will not slumber nor sleep.
>
> PSALM 121:3

Date: _____

Prayer and Response

Heavenly Father, today I will dwell on...

_____
_____
_____
_____
_____
_____
_____
_____
_____
_____
_____
_____
_____
_____
_____
_____

Look at the birds of the air; they do not sow or reap or store away in barns, and yet your heavenly Father feeds them. Are you not much more valuable than they?

MATTHEW 6:26

Date: _____

Prayer and Response

Heavenly Father, today I will pause with...

> You will keep her in perfect peace, whose mind is stayed on You, because she trusts in You. Trust in the LORD forever for in God the LORD we have an everlasting rock.
>
> ISAIAH 26:3-4

Date: _____

_____
_____
_____
_____
_____
_____
_____
_____
_____
_____
_____
_____
_____
_____
_____

Prayer and Response

Heavenly Father, today I will linger with…

_____

_____

_____

_____

_____

_____

_____

_____

_____

_____

_____

_____

_____

_____

_____

_____

_____

> Because you have been my help, therefor in the shadow of Your wings I will rejoice. My soul clings hard to You; Your right hand upholds me.
>
> PSALM 63:7-8

Date: _____

_____
_____
_____
_____
_____
_____
_____
_____
_____
_____
_____
_____
_____
_____
_____
_____
_____

Prayer and Response

Heavenly Father, today I will rest with...

_____
_____
_____
_____
_____
_____
_____
_____
_____
_____
_____
_____
_____
_____
_____
_____

She Anchors Her Confidence in the Faithfulness of Her God

DEUTERONOMY 31:6

Be strong and courageous. Do not be afraid or terrified because of them, for the LORD your God goes with you; He will never leave you – He will not forsake you.

WHAT IS THIS SCRIPTURE SPREAKING TO ME?

_____
_____
_____
_____
_____
_____

HOW DO I APPLY THE SCRIPTURE TO MY LIFE?

_____
_____
_____
_____
_____
_____

PSALM 56:3

When I am afraid, I put my trust in you.

WHAT IS THIS SCRIPTURE SPREAKING TO ME?

_____
_____
_____
_____
_____
_____

HOW DO I APPLY THE SCRIPTURE TO MY LIFE?

_____
_____
_____
_____
_____
_____
_____

LUKE 1:37

For nothing will be impossible with God.

WHAT IS THIS SCRIPTURE SPREAKING TO ME?

_____
_____
_____
_____
_____
_____

HOW DO I APPLY THE SCRIPTURE TO MY LIFE?

_____
_____
_____
_____
_____
_____
_____

PHILIPPIANS 4:19

My God will meet your every need out of His riches in the glory that is found in Christ Jesus.

WHAT IS THIS SCRIPTURE SPREAKING TO ME?

_____
_____
_____
_____
_____

HOW DO I APPLY THE SCRIPTURE TO MY LIFE?

_____
_____
_____
_____
_____
_____

PHILIPPIANS 4:6

Be anxious or worry about nothing, but in everything by prayer and supplication, with thanksgiving, let your request be made known to God.

WHAT IS THIS SCRIPTURE SPREAKING TO ME?

_____
_____
_____
_____
_____
_____

HOW DO I APPLY THE SCRIPTURE TO MY LIFE?

_____
_____
_____
_____
_____
_____

PROVERBS 18:10

The name of the LORD is a strong tower; The righteous run to it and are safe.

WHAT IS THIS SCRIPTURE SPREAKING TO ME?

_____
_____
_____
_____
_____
_____

HOW DO I APPLY THE SCRIPTURE TO MY LIFE?

_____
_____
_____
_____
_____
_____
_____

PSALM 91:1-2

He who dwells in the shelter of the Most High shall abide under the shadow of the Almighty. I will say of the LORD, He is my refuge and my fortress my God in whom I trust.

WHAT IS THIS SCRIPTURE SPREAKING TO ME?

_____
_____
_____
_____
_____
_____

HOW DO I APPLY THE SCRIPTURE TO MY LIFE?

_____
_____
_____
_____
_____
_____

PSALM 46:1

God is our refuge and strength, a very present help in trouble.

WHAT IS THIS SCRIPTURE SPEAKING TO ME?

_____
_____
_____
_____
_____

HOW DO I APPLY THE SCRIPTURE TO MY LIFE?

_____
_____
_____
_____
_____
_____
_____

PHILIPPIANS 4:13

I can do all things through Christ which strengthens me.

WHAT IS THIS SCRIPTURE SPREAKING TO ME?

_____
_____
_____
_____
_____
_____

HOW DO I APPLY THE SCRIPTURE TO MY LIFE?

_____
_____
_____
_____
_____
_____

www.ingramcontent.com/pod-product-compliance
Lightning Source LLC
Chambersburg PA
CBHW071409290426
44108CB00014B/1742